Werner Lantermann, Susanne Lantermann
and Julie Mancini

Cockatoos

Everything About Purchase, Care,
Nutrition, Behavior, and Breeding

BARRON'S

CONTENTS

CONSIDERATIONS BEFORE BUYING

Cockatoos are boisterous, playful pets that need a lot of time and attention from their owners. They are playful, clever pets that offer hours of entertainment and companionship. These intelligent birds also require large cages and ample opportunities for play and exercise.

This Is the Cockatoo

Cockatoo, a Malaysian word, has been said to mean "old Father" or "pincer"—the latter meaning being quite clear to anyone who has ever felt the sharp beak of a cockatoo. Yet, when properly cared for, these sociable parrots are the most lovable of all creatures, whose endless inventiveness and extraordinary playfulness enchant an ever-increasing number of cockatoo owners.

Cockatoos are different from other parrots in looks as well as in behavior:

Plumage: Their single-colored plumage, usually white or dark, bears a healthy coating of power. Cockatoos are almost unique among birds in their possession of a mobile crest. The crests of the various species of cockatoos are said to be recumbent (curving back) or recurve (curving forward at the tip). Cockatoos also possess cheek feathers that can completely cover their beaks and ear coverts when they are erected as part of a facial display. As a result, cockatoos have the most expressive faces of any bird. Indeed, the facial display of a male Moluccan cockatoo, including crest, facial fan, and ear coverts, can be fully one half of his total body height![1]

Devotion (bonding): More than any other parrots, companion cockatoos can become so attached to an individual that separation becomes almost impossible without emotional injury to the cockatoo. That special person must pay a great deal of attention to the cockatoo every day. This requires committing much time to filling the more or less involuntary role of a partner.

[1]Murphy, James J. *Cockatoos Are Different Because They Have Crests.* White Mt. Bird Firm, Inc., 1998.

═══ TIP ═══

Imitation Is the Highest Form of Flattery

Chi-Chi is a large umbrella cockatoo who lives with a mature couple. As there are no children in the home, both Lonnie and Anja spend a great deal of time with Chi-Chi. Some afternoons, the bird is allowed to join Lonnie as he plies his woodworking hobby in the garage. Chi-Chi watches from the safety of a Plexiglas cage while Lonnie works with power tools: saws, drills, and sanders.

One afternoon they all took a break, removing the bird from the Plexiglas enclosure, as the couple shared iced tea. The bird hopped blissfully from arm to bench to table to saw, at one point picking up a small block of wood. As Lonnie and Anja watched, Chi-Chi carefully applied the wooden block to the circular blade of the table saw, as he had seen Lonnie do so many times. The bird eyeballed the blade with interest and obvious disappointment as nothing happened. Chi-Chi reapplied the block of wood to the blade, and again seeing no result, resorted to the traditional means of reshaping wood. He simply chewed the block to splinters.

Several complications can result from this bonding scenario: 1) aggression related to jealousy can result in injuries to humans; and 2) an extremely human-bonded cockatoo will get used to a cockatoo mate only with the greatest difficulty and may be incapable of reproducing.

Playfulness and Loud Cries: Almost all cockatoo species demonstrate extraordinary playfulness and inventiveness. A typical companion cockatoo improvises many games, tricks, shaking and climbing exercises, or the use of various objects as tools. Such activities are carried out all day long without interruption, except for brief rest periods, so that the birds are in almost constant motion. Cockatoos accompany their play with loud screams, which in the larger species can sometimes escalate to a deafening, prolonged shriek.

Beak Shape and Strength: Many cockatoo beaks can break human flesh in three places simultaneously because of dual points on the mandible (lower beak) and a single point on the maxilla (upper beak). Additionally, the enormous power of the cockatoo should not go unmentioned. Scarcely any other of the large parrot species can do as much mischief with its beak as the cockatoo. With ease it demolishes objects such as ordinary plastic food dishes, for example, not to mention the whittling away of perches. The larger cockatoos are also able to bend the bars of the ordinary parrot cage in a very short time and crack the joints. Therefore additional security is advised for cage doors. Buying a suitable, stable (and therefore, usually, expensive) cage is a prerequisite for keeping cockatoos.

Avoid cages that have a guillotine type door. The name explains it all. These doors open up and down, and if the cockatoo's activities loosen the device that holds the door open and in position it can fall on the bird and do serious damage.

Cockatoos are extremely intelligent and dexterous. Do not rely on the simple closing and locking devices that come with most cages.

Add a combination lock to be sure that your cockatoos will not open the door to the cage and investigate the rest of the house while you are away.

Ability to Mimic: Cockatoos have never been known as outstanding talkers but they are capable of speech and other forms of mimicry. Their real skills, however, are based on their intelligence. It is not unusual for a cockatoo that was a handfed baby to greet its owner with a charming "hello" or to say "good-bye" at just the right moment. Many cockatoos can be taught to dance in a rhythmic response to singing or music as well as to roller skate or even play tug o' war.

Considerations Before Buying a Cockatoo

When you've become somewhat familiar with the cockatoo's character traits and decide that keeping one might be possible, think carefully about the following points:

✔ Companion cockatoos require a great deal of attention. The ever more intense animal-human relationship generates a time-consuming and unpredictable responsibility, which some people are not able to handle over the long term.

✔ For feeding a single cockatoo, plan on spending an average of 20 to 30 minutes per day. This involves preparing the food, cleaning the feed dishes and the cage surroundings inside the house, as well as daily dusting, for cockatoos regularly produce feather dust.

✔ The loud voice of a cockatoo can lead to difficulties, especially if you live in an apartment. Find out ahead of time if your neighbors can comfortably tolerate a parrot being kept nearby. Don't forget to tell them that some cockatoos scream even in the dark, a characteristic that is almost unheard-of in other parrots.

✔ During vacation or in case you are ill, the cockatoo should be cared for by someone it already knows. You must plan ahead for this.

✔ The cost of buying a fully-weaned cockatoo, proper medical care, and the proper equipment for keeping one can be quite expensive.

✔ Unless you have had experience in hand-feeding a baby parrot, do not consider purchasing an unweaned cockatoo. There is danger to the baby bird if you are not capable of feeding it successfully enough to fill its crop at regular intervals with food of the proper consistency and at the proper temperature. Of course, there are great rewards if you do complete handfeeding a baby cockatoo as it will bond with you for life and consider you to be the equivalent of its parent.

Considerations Before Buying a Second Cockatoo

Sometimes a cockatoo does not adjust well to a particular environment without the presence of another cockatoo. This need for "cockatoo-specific culture" can be addressed by the addition of another cockatoo. Two cockatoos who get along well together make fewer demands on the keeper's time because they are not so dependent on the keeper's attention as a single bird would be.

The burden of noise will naturally be much greater when you have more than one bird. Especially if you are keeping cockatoos in an outdoor aviary, their cries can lead to trouble with noise-sensitive neighbors.

The daily time needed for cleaning and care increases with two birds. The time expenditure for preparing food can be even greater if you want to breed cockatoos (see page 53).

Keeping more than two cockatoos is especially interesting for the cockatoo fancier who has breeding in mind. In this case, the construction of a bird room or an aviary and bird shelter (page 24) is recommended.

Cockatoos and Other Parrots

Other Parrots of the Same Size: Cockatoos usually get along fairly well with other parrots of the same size if there are enough opportunities for freedom of movement inside the cage or aviary. However, you should never add a third bird to an already established pair of cockatoos. It would most likely be harassed by the male, chased, and sooner or later would have to be separated from the pair.

Smaller Parakeets and Parrot Species: We do not consider such combinations advisable. The smaller psittacines are apt to quickly fall prey to the strong beak of the cockatoo.

Cockatoos and Other Pets

Dogs and Cats: In some cases cockatoos get along well with these other pets, if both parties are allowed gradually to get used to each other. Cats, for example, after one uncomfortable encounter with the strong cockatoo

What Does a Companion Cockatoo Really Need?

Before you decide to purchase a companion cockatoo, it is important to realize what it will need. The following is a description of the two basics:

I. Education

A successful companion cockatoo must learn:

✔ *Appropriate Interactive Behavior.* Cockatoos are famously interactive, but many of them prefer cuddling, cuddling, or cuddling. They are capable of demanding this preference in extremely obtrusive ways, perhaps screaming for attention, perhaps biting when being picked up or put down. Successful companion cockatoos must be guided to develop routine and predictable cooperative interactions, including step-ups, playing peek-a-boo, and retiring peacefully for the evening.

✔ *Independent Behavior.* Failure to develop independent behaviors can be devastating to a cockatoo's successful long-term adjustment in companion settings. A cockatoo that does not learn to play happily alone with toys, chew wood, or disassemble puzzles might instead spend time playing with or chewing its own feathers, or jangling human nerves and eardrums with attention-demanding calls.

II. Accommodation

A successful companion cockatoo must have:

✔ *A Rich, Stimulating Environment, Including Quality Diet, Equipment, and Housing.* Cockatoos require exceptionally strong cages and an ever-changing variety of interesting toys. They need a well-planned and delivered diet and perches in diverse sizes and textures. Like other parrots, cockatoos need full spectrum lighting and access to fresh water for drinking and bathing.

✔ *Clean Quarters.* Healthy cockatoos produce lots of powder and need to be able to reduce wood and other destructible chewables to small splinters. During warm weather, they shed and replace feathers almost continuously. Cockatoos like to throw things; they often store and soak things in their water bowls; and they must, of course, poop. Optimum health and behavior are best retained in well-maintained environments, so cockatoos must live with industrious and accommodating humans who are willing to clean up after them.

✔ *Tolerant Humans.* Cockatoos are darling but demanding. Successful cockatoo families must be able to accommodate a little screaming every now and again; a little nipping, sometimes; and occasional demolition of human possessions. A happy cockatoo will be exploratory and curious, and will wish to communicate a wide variety of wonderful discoveries and emotions to treasured humans. Successful cockatoo families are loving and accepting, for cockatoos are not unlike toddlers who never grow up.

beak, often make a wide circuit around a parrot cage. However, harmonious relationships among dogs, cats, and large parrots are occasionally cited in newspapers. You have to try to see what works and what doesn't in your own situation. Some dogs and most ferrets can be too predatory to safely interact with a cockatoo.

Other Small Pets: Direct contact with cockatoos frequently ends in fatality for small mammals like guinea pigs, hamsters, or mice. Smaller birds like zebra finches or canaries will also quickly fall prey to a cockatoo.

Cockatoos and Children

Babies and small children must never be left alone with a cockatoo that has the freedom of the house. If a baby competes for what was once the cockatoo's position as favorite, the bird may react with jealousy, attacking the child.

Older children and teenagers, however, can gradually become familiar with the habits of a cockatoo. At the same time, they can also learn how to assume responsibility for a companion parrot, which requires regular care and feeding and must never be neglected.

ADVICE ON BUYING A COCKATOO

Purchasing the right cockatoo can make all the difference between an enjoyable pet and a problem animal. You are already taking an important first step by reading this book and doing some research prior to bringing a bird home. Make arrangements to see birds at several breeders or bird specialty stores before making your final decision.

Where to Buy a Cockatoo

Pet Shop or Breeder: If you are a first-time parrot keeper, it's a good idea to get your cockatoo from a well-respected source such as a breeder or pet store with a good reputation for supplying healthy, well-adjusted chicks. No cockatoos have been imported into the United States since 1992, so all baby cockatoos sold legally in the United States since that time were hatched in captivity. Expect a premium, fully-weaned, handfed baby cockatoo from a primary source to be expensive—it's worth it! Some bird fanciers have breeding pairs of birds that produce lovely and healthy baby cockatoos, but the breeder chooses not to hand feed them because of the amount of work involved. When you go to purchase a baby cockatoo make sure that it has been hand fed by the breeder rather than having been left in the cage with its parents. A cockatoo baby that is not hand fed will take longer to tame when you get it.

Newspaper Advertisements: A more experienced cockatoo buyer may find success buying a "resale" bird from the newspaper. A young cockatoo (under four years old) that has had only one home may still be a premium prospect as a companion cockatoo. Unfortunately, some resale cockatoos have suffered "behavioral damage" as a result of being poorly socialized, unsocialized, neglected, or otherwise abused.

Parrot Rescue Groups: Parrot rescue groups provide temporary homes for unwanted birds. Check with groups in your area for a homeless cockatoo, then invest a lot of love and patience in your bird as it settles into your home.

Choosing a Healthy Cockatoo

Proper evaluation of a cockatoo's health is impossible for a layperson, and no cockatoo should be purchased without being examined by an experienced avian veterinarian, either before or after the sale.

The following checklist may help you in evaluating a bird while making your selection:

Housing: Cages and aviaries with thick layers of droppings, dirty interior fittings, feeding dishes containing rancid food or inadequate diets, and dirty drinking water may be prime evidence of poor bird care. Poor care can easily affect the health and disposition of cockatoo chicks.

Appearance of the Birds: Look for a baby cockatoo that is still handfeeding. Handfeeding babies may have a few soiled feathers, but if plumage is grown in, it should be uniform, symmetrical, and intact. If feathers are not yet opened, look for sharply pointed spikes rather than rounded unopened feathers, which may be an indication of severe, incurable, and contagious disease (Psittacine Beak and Feather Disease, also called PBFD). Baby cockatoos will have black eyes and soft, almost flexible beaks.

A healthy, fully-weaned juvenile or adult cockatoo will have powder on the feathers. Rubbing the crest or other large feathers between thumb and forefinger should leave a slick powder coating on the fingers. Nostrils should be dry and clear. Eyes should be round (not slitted), clear, and shining. Generally a sick cockatoo has an apathetic, distressed appearance. It sleeps a great deal, rests on both legs—in contrast to a healthy (adult) bird—and takes little or no nourishment. Missing claws

or missing toes are beauty flaws, not signs of illness, which occur rarely in handfed domestic cockatoos. A cockatoo purchased for breeding should have a complete set of claws. A cockatoo that lacks a full set of claws will not be able to remain steady on the perch during copulation. This will inhibit the bird's ability to successfully engage in breeding.

Droppings: The droppings of a healthy bird consist of olive green and white urates, and should be medium firm and formed. Unformed, watery, different-colored, or even bloody stool can be an indication of illness.

Behavior: During the brief buying encounter, it's hardly possible to tell whether a cockatoo has potential for behavioral maladjustment. Almost all baby cockatoos are cuddly and snuggly, and so a bird's potential to develop behavior problems cannot usually be determined. However, excessively noisy begging or obvious fearfulness can be a sign of potential behavioral problems in handfeeding baby cockatoos.

Determining Gender

In a few of the white cockatoo species, gender can be easily determined in mature birds. Of the species discussed in this book, the females of the Lesser Sulphur-crested, Greater Sulphur-crested, and Umbrella cockatoos can display a brown, chestnut-brown, or red-brown iris color. The iris of the mature male cockatoo of these species is dark brown to black.

Laparascopic surgical sexing is still sometimes performed by experienced veterinarians if there is some question about a bird's internal condition. DNA analysis is the best, the least invasive, most dependable scientific technique for deter-

mining gender. This procedure can be done with a mail-in kit with samples of blood feathers or a few drops of blood from a toenail.

Determining Age

Cockatoos are among the longest lived of the parrots. Although there are stories of cockatoos living for more than one hundred years, these are always poorly documented and generally result from some member of the family forgetting that a new bird was purchased when the old one died at the ripe old age of 40 or 50 years. A cockatoo that is properly fed and given plenty of exercise can easily reach 50 to 60 years of age.

The plumage of the old bird has all the typical markings (see species descriptions, page 69). In young birds, the yellow cheek patch, for example, or the yellow crest color (in Lesser and Greater Sulphur-crested cockatoos) is paler. The plumage of young Rose-breasted cockatoos is duller all over. Young Greater Sulphur-crested cockatoos and Umbrella-crested cockatoos often show pale gray shadows in the plumage.

The iris color undergoes a color change over the course of several months and years. In adult female cockatoos, the iris is usually intense red or red-brown in color, whereas in birds under two years old, as a rule, it is dark brown or yellow-brown.

The beak of a young bird is shiny and smooth, and without the visible stratifications that develop with the growth of horn in older parrots.

The feet of younger cockatoos display a somewhat more widely spread scale structure.

In the first weeks of life, young birds rest on both feet and only later adopt the typical one-legged sleeping and resting position.

Formalities of Purchase

When buying a cockatoo, various legal regulations must be observed. The overall guiding principle is the Washington agreement, the Convention on International Trade in Endangered Species (CITES) of Wild Flora and Fauna (hereafter referred to as WA), which comprehensively lists all animal and plant species that are threatened, endangered, or threatened with extinction. The agreement is divided into three categories (Appendices I through III). All cockatoo species (with the exception of the Palm cockatoo, which is listed in Appendix I and is one of the animal species threatened with extinction) are entered in Appendix II of the WA, which lists those species that are under special regulation but that may still be bought and sold. Of course, wild-caught birds may not be imported into the United States.

Leg Band: The band is the legal identification for the bird. It helps to document transfers of ownership as well as proof of ownership, when necessary.

Sales Contract: Some states require that the sale of a psittacine bird be documented and reported to the state agency tracking parrot sales. Additionally, most sales contracts specify length and details of health guarantees as well as documenting age and, in some cases, parentage of the birds.

HOUSING AND EQUIPMENT

Before you bring your cockatoo home, have its cage set up and move-in ready. Your bird will also need a few more accessories, such as spare sets of dishes and perches. Your pet may also enjoy an indoor climbing tree as an additional place to play and climb outside its cage.

Keeping a Cockatoo Indoors

Indoor Cage Size: Because they are so active, the small companion cockatoos need just as just as much cage space as the larger ones. For a single bird or for temporary accommodation of a pair, the cage must have a floor surface area of at least 27 × 27 inches (70 × 70 cm) and a height of 39 inches (100 cm). Breeding cages are probably best set up as flights that are longer—at least 4 to 6 feet (120 to 180 cm)—rather than taller.

Cage Shape: A companion parrot cage should be square, with a right-angled base; round cages are unsuitable.

Bars: At least two sides of the cage bars should be horizontal so that the cockatoo can climb readily, and the gauge should be heavy enough so that the bird can't bend the bars with its strong beak.

Tray: Commercially available parrot cages have trays for catching droppings that can be pulled out like a drawer. If the bird can get to the tray, it's better off made with galvanized steel.

Cage Door: The cage door should be large enough so that the parrot can go in and out easily on a human hand, without having to lower the crest. Some cockatoos learn very quickly how to open the cage door with their beaks, so it is advisable to secure the door with a combination lock.

The Bird Room

A bird room is almost the ideal setup for keeping cockatoos. For this you need an empty room with windows, in which the cockatoos can move freely without any cage boundaries.

However, such a room needs careful preparation to make it suitable for cockatoos:

✔ All carpets and wall and ceiling coverings must be removed.

✔ Walls and ceiling must be covered with a nontoxic coat of whitewash or latex paint (available from a paint dealer), or be tiled.

✔ Doors, heating units, exposed electrical wires, electrical outlets, light switches, and light fixtures should be covered with tin or wire mesh.

✔ It is a good idea to seal the floor so that no dampness can seep through to rooms underneath.

✔ Wooden floors or carpeted floors should be converted to tile.

✔ The amount of equipment needed depends on the number of birds: climbing trees (see page 23), bathing pans, a feeding board with removable dishes, and nest boxes (page 54).

Advantages of this type of room include:

✔ The cockatoos live in a controlled, evenly maintained climate.

✔ The loud voices of the cockatoos are not so audible to neighbors living nearby.

✔ There is less danger of theft.

Disadvantages include:

✔ The parrots receive only a limited amount of daylight.

✔ Full spectrum lighting must be provided.

✔ "Rainfall" in the form of daily showers must be provided.

Equipment for Cages and Aviaries

Perches: Use round perches with a diameter of about 1 inch (25 to 30 mm) for smaller cockatoos (see description of species, page 69); for larger species the diameter should be 1½ to 2 inches (35 to 45 mm). It's good to have the perches of varying thicknesses so that muscles are exercised and the birds' feet don't go lame. The branches of unsprayed fruit trees (after being carefully scrubbed under hot running water) make excellent perches. Their rough upper surfaces are good for wearing down the claws of the cockatoos by natural means, as well as for foot exercises. Perches need to be mounted in the cage so that the bowls for water and food will not be fouled by the falling droppings of the birds.

Food and Water Dishes: When you buy a parrot cage, ordinary plastic food and water bowls are usually included. Plastic dishes will be gnawed to pieces by the cockatoos in a short time and must then be changed. Better food and water dishes are those made of pottery or stainless steel, which can be fastened in the cage, aviary, or bird room with special holders (all available from the pet dealer). There should be a total of three dishes (see page 42).

Bathing Pans: Cockatoos like to bathe to get rid of feather dust. Shallow clay flowerpot saucers with a diameter of 12 to 14 inches (30 to 35 cm) are excellent for this purpose.

Play and Exercise Equipment: Chains with large links, climbing ropes, fresh branches for gnawing, and wooden parrot toys present the single bird as well as aviary birds with opportunities to exercise and provide variety in their caged existence; they also serve to maintain the condition of beak and claws.

Caution: Do not use any branches from poisonous trees or shrubs! For example, acacia,

apple, cherry, yew, laburnum, viburnum, black honeysuckle, holly, dwarf elder, and many evergreens are all poisonous.

Calcium Block: It's pointless to put a calcium block into some cockatoo cages. The birds will peck it to pieces within minutes and throw it on the floor. The remains are then ignored completely. Since the advent of modern scientifically formulated diets, we no longer need to add vitamins and minerals to our bird's diets at all unless the veterinarian detects a special condition requiring supplementation.

Substratum: In recent years, Dr. Susan Clubb, an avian veterinarian from Florida, has reported university studies that demonstrate that newspaper with print is the best material tested to line the bottom of bird cages. She reports that the ink in the newspaper appears to retard the growth of bacteria, fungus, and molds more than any other material tested.

Do not use corncob, cedar shavings, cat litter, or sand as cage substrates. They do not absorb cage waste. They may also harm your cockatoo's health. Either your bird can become ill by ingesting the substrate or the substrate may create a medium for bacterial growth.

Placement of Cage or Aviary: Choose a quiet corner of the living area that is easily seen from most areas of this space so that the cockatoo can take part in the life of the family and will not become bored. Never put the cage directly on the floor. This makes the cockatoo feel insecure. Many domestic companion cockatoos develop territorial behaviors if they are housed high, and may bite humans that are shorter than they. It's best to house a companion domestic cockatoo no higher than the height of the shortest person. In homes where children or very short adults are present, a small stepladder can assist even the shortest family member in retrieving a well-socialized cockatoo from the top of the cage.

Free Flight in the House

Freedom to fly about the house is especially dangerous for cockatoos. While it offers excitement and opportunity for exercise, it is generally considered too dangerous in these days of ceiling fans and many-tentacled electrical appliances. Companion parrots should be safely and sensitively groomed to prevent indoor flight (see page 36).

Caution: Remove all houseplants so that the cockatoo can't nibble or eat them. Otherwise poisoning and death might result.

Open Perch or Indoor Climbing Tree

Under supervision, hand-tame cockatoos can be kept during the day for hours at a time on a free perch or climbing tree. It's a pleasant change for the cockatoo, and the keeper can then enjoy watching the acrobatic skills of his bird. The parrot should spend the rest of the time in its cage and it should be fed there. In time, the bird develops a regular daily rhythm. Eventually it will return voluntarily to its cage with hunger and the onset of darkness. Tame, wing-feather-trimmed cockatoos enjoy daily transportation to and from the cage as a guaranteed amount of human attention they will receive.

Open Perch: The simplest form of open perch indoors is one that is fastened onto the top of the cage. It should be mounted approximately 6 inches (15 cm) above the roof and should not extend to the side beyond the cage measurements, so that the bird droppings will fall into the cage and not onto the floor. The opportunities for the cockatoo to exercise on such a perch are quite limited, however.

Climbing Tree: For a climbing tree you need a flowerpot filled with sand or a cement pot (diameter about 39 inches [100 cm]; height about 7½ inches [50 cm]) and a well-branched limb. To keep the branch upright in the container, dampen the sand somewhat before you put it in the container and then tamp it down well. Of course you can also purchase suitable climbing trees in many pet stores. The more

chances to climb that the tree offers, the better for the cockatoo.

Warning: Improperly fastened perches or ones that break suddenly can injure the bird or even kill it with a fall.

Keeping Cockatoos Outdoors

A bird shelter with a garden flight cage attached offers the cockatoos the best possible quality of life they can enjoy in human captivity.

The parrots have light, air, sun, rain, and opportunities to dig, fly, or climb. If you plan to allow breeding and to keep several cockatoos, this form of housing or a bird room is highly recommended.

HOW–TO: BUILD A BIRD

Your building plans must allow for several basic considerations:

✔ Find out about local building regulations and whether a building permit is necessary.

✔ Use only very strong construction materials, ones that can stand up under the strong beaks of the cockatoos.

✔ The bird shelter should be built of brick or stone and sit on a solid cement foundation. Good insulation saves on heating.

✔ The use of simple transparent glass bricks for windows is ideal.

✔ The fly-through to the flight cage is created with a glass-brick-equipped aluminum swivel window (size about 19½ × 9¾ inches [50 × 25 cm]).

✔ Ceramic tiles are particularly good for covering the walls and floor because they are easy to clean and can't be easily destroyed by cockatoo beaks.

✔ Heating, light (fluorescents), and running water are essential features for the bird shelter.

✔ The size of the inside space: a floor surface of 72 × 24 inches (186 × 62 cm) and 48 inches (124 cm) in height is enough for a pair of cockatoos.

✔ The equipment for the interior consists of a feeding board with removable dishes, several perches, and a nest box.

Note: Besides conforming to code requirements, the proposed aviary and bird shelter should be approved as to their suitability for proper maintenance of the birds.

The flight cage should be attached to the shelter so that the cockatoos can leave

their inner room even in bad weather. The following points must be considered when you are building the flight cage:

✔ It is advisable to lay a cement foundation (being careful to observe building codes).

✔ If you are handy with tools you can make the cage supports yourself from galvanized steel pipes (bolted or welded).

✔ It's best to use galvanized wire mesh for fencing. Mesh size of 0.8 × 0.8 inches (19 × 19 mm) and wire gauge of 0.04 to 0.06 inches (1.05 to 1.50 mm) will do for small cockatoos; for larger birds use mesh size of 2 × 2 inches (50 × 50 mm) and wire gauge of 0.16 inches (4 mm).

✔ Rats, mice, and other small mammals carry disease or even kill cockatoos if they get into the aviary. Therefore, be sure to secure the fencing with a small enough mesh size.

✔ A third of the flight should be roofed to offer the cockatoos shelter from too much rain or sun.

✔ Paving flags are especially good for the flight cage floor. Many cockatoos like to scratch and dig in the ground; you can add a thick layer of sand.

✔ For the entrance to the flight cage, it is recommended that you make a small outer door that is secured, and allow a space and a second door, like an air lock, to keep the cockatoos from escaping.

✔ The equipment for the aviary consists of climbing trees, baths, and several perches (see page 23).

ACCLIMATION AND CARE

Cockatoo care is not particularly difficult, but it does require a daily commitment from you, the owner. Your bird will need to have its food and water dishes changed and refilled daily, and the cage will need to be cleaned weekly. Your pet will also need daily one-on-one time with you in addition to opportunities for independent play.

Taking Your Bird Home

After your neonatal (unweaned) cockatoo becomes a juvenile or fully weaned bird, you can take it home safely in a car in a rigid carrier. The bird should not be loose in the car, as this can lead to car accidents. Even the most inconsequential accident that doesn't injure humans can easily injure a loose bird in the car.

Ideally, the cage the bird has been in should be taken home, or one identical to it should await the bird, fully furnished in the new home. Try to bring the baby home early in the day, so that it has time to become accustomed to its cage in the new surroundings. A very young (under six months old) cockatoo might prefer to spend the night in the carrier, rather than be introduced to an unfamiliar cage late in the day.

You will have a window of opportunity of two days to six months during which an exuberant young cockatoo will willingly cooperate with patterning exercises such as step-up and towel peek-a-boo's. (See Hand-taming on page 28 for details on teaching the step-up command.) During this same time period, a young cockatoo must also learn independent play habits.

During this period you should:

✔ Provide the cockatoo with peace and give it time to get to know its new environment.

✔ Keep visitors and resident pets well away from it.

✔ Maintain the recommended diet from the person from whom the bird was purchased, or correct the diet (see Diet, page 39).

✔ Take the bird, as quickly as possible, to an experienced avian veterinarian for an examination and blood tests to verify the bird's health.

✔ Practice stepping the bird from hand to hand to pattern cooperation.

✔ Play peek-a-boo in a towel to get the bird used to restraint for grooming and examinations.
✔ Observe the bird's behavior to ensure that it is interested and lively and develops natural curiosity rather than focusing on one person and his attentions.
✔ Provide a variety of toys as tools for the development of independent play behaviors.

Placement in an Aviary

A cockatoo that is intended for an aviary is always first introduced into the bird shelter. Such a bird should have full wings and flight capacity. If possible, first place the parrot in a separate section inside the shelter so that it can get comfortable with its new surroundings. With a mature cockatoo, particularly, great care must be taken to integrate the bird into an already established aviary community. The connecting hatch to the flight cage should not be opened until a cockatoo has become familiar with the dimensions of the bird shelter, finds the perches without great difficulty, and regularly visits the feeding dish.

Some birds must be placed in the flight cage and brought back into the shelter again before they learn to find the way by themselves.

Hand-taming

Hand-tamed describes a parrot that willingly steps up, without biting, onto your hand upon request. To achieve and maintain this requires practice in a happy, cooperative interaction. A newly-weaned juvenile cockatoo should enjoy practicing the step-up routine for at least a minute or two on most days. The bird's enjoyment of the interaction is the most important part.

While a very young cockatoo will probably willingly cooperate almost anyplace with anything involving touch, you might have to begin step-up practice with an older bird in unfamiliar territory. A laundry room or hallway is usually perfect, as the bird will probably never spend much time in these areas, and therefore should not develop territorial behavior in them. Step-up practice should include practice stepping the bird from the hand to and from an unfamiliar perch, practice stepping the bird from hand to hand, practice stepping the bird from a hand-held perch to and from an unfamiliar perch, practice stepping the bird from a hand-held perch to a hand-held perch, and practice stepping the bird from a familiar perch to and from both hands and to and from hand-held perches.

Be sure to offer affection and praise after each completed step-up. Always discontinue step-up practice only after a successful completion of the command. This is crucial to good patterning. If the command is not successful, alter technique, approach, or prompting mannerisms rather than continue with unsuccessful methods. Be careful not to reinforce unsuccessful patterns.

There is no substitute for warm, genuine human enthusiasm as a reward for the bird's success in stepping up. Especially with shy or cautious birds, the bird's enjoyment of the process is essential. If the bird is not eagerly, or at least willingly, cooperating with step-ups and step-up practice, something is going wrong, and the owner should find professional help immediately.

Intensive contact with humans is extremely important for the single bird because the cockatoo has a great need for social contact (for a partner). With the onset of sexual maturity this need becomes even stronger. Without appropriate behavioral training to be both interactive and independent, a neglected cockatoo can easily respond by beginning to scream, or pulling out its feathers.

Learning to "Talk"

Speaking, or more correctly, the imitation of human words is, for parrots, a form of making contact with their caretakers. All large parrots possess the ability (some more, some less) to imitate words or various sounds. In general, cockatoos do not master this skill to a high degree, but through patient schooling you can eventually succeed in training any cockatoo to produce one or another word or short phrases.

Vowels (a, e, i, o, u) usually can be imitated better than consonants or sibilants.

If You Keep Two Cockatoos Indoors

Some people believe that keeping a pair of cockatoos that are bonded to each other rather than to humans is easier than keeping just one cockatoo. The jury is still out on that one. Usually a cockatoo owner already has one bird before deciding to get a second. Of course it isn't entirely easy to bring two strange parrots together. Be sure to choose a bird of the opposite sex (see Determining Gender, page 15) of the same cockatoo species or subspecies. Many times you may thus get a harmonious pair that may even breed in the right circumstances. It's rarely a good idea to pair up two cockatoos of the same sex, or different species.

Getting Used to Each Other: Never put two strange birds together right off. First the cockatoos should observe and get to know cach other—separated by a cage wall—for several days or weeks. Only then do you bring both parrots together on neutral ground, that is, not in the cage of the established bird, and observe their behavior. If the pair is compatible, the mood of the cockatoos is easy to determine by the fanning of the tail or the erection of the crest (see Courtship and Mating, page 55). If the meeting continues without any disturbances, they may remain together in the same cage; otherwise they should be separated and the attempt repeated later until both birds come to an agreement. This should not take more than three or four attempts. If it does, you may want to reconsider the match.

Note: A single bird loses a little of its original tameness as it turns more to its mate than to its caretaker. Pairs that get along well together can often be left completely alone, because they can keep each other occupied.

Cleaning the Bird Shelter and the Flight Cage

Daily: Remove leftover food; clean feed and water dishes with hot water, dry, and refill.

Weekly: Rake out earth and sand substrate and, if necessary, spread a layer of clean sand.

Monthly: The perches will be gnawed away relatively quickly by the cockatoos' strong beaks. Thus, regular changing of perches is required. Storing natural branches is advisable.

Every Six Months: Completely change the floor litter; scrub the floor of the flight cage, disinfect, and spread with a layer of clean sand.

Yearly: Major cleaning; wash down even the flight caging and the walls of the bird shelter. If necessary, apply a new layer of paint.

Important: During the cleaning and disinfection, the parrots must be removed to another place and returned to the aviary when the shelter is dry.

Table of Dangers

Source of Danger	Consequences	How to Avoid
Adhesives	Poisoning with fatal outcome caused by volatile solvents.	Remove all animals from the room when using adhesives (repairing, model-making, laying floors) and ventilate very well after the work is finished.
Bathroom	Escaping through opened window. Drowning by falling into open toilet, sink, or tub. Poisoning from cleaning materials and chemicals.	Keep parrots out of the bathroom; never leave the bathroom door open. Maintain wing-feather trims.
Cage Wire	Strangling or getting stuck in grill with openings that are too large. Injuries to toes and head on thin, sharp-edged wire.	Choose a mesh size and a wire gauge that are appropriate for the size of the bird and examine the cage regularly for loose parts and changes caused by the bird and use over time.
Ceiling fans	Birds allowed to fly indoors crash into spinning blades.	Install protective grill or shield access to fan. Maintain wing-feather trims.
Doors	Caught or crushed in a carelessly closed or opened door. Escaping.	Accidents and escape can be avoided only with the greatest vigilance. Maintain wing-feather trims.
Drafts	Colds.	Avoid drafts as much as possible; set up a windbreak in an outdoor aviary.
Electric wires	Shock from gnawing or biting through wires; often fatal.	Conceal wires under trim and carpets and behind furniture, or cover with metal shields; pull plugs. Maintain wing-feather trims.

Table of Dangers (continued)

Source of Danger	Consequences	How to Avoid
Kitchen	Steam can seriously injure and fumes (especially burning plastics) can kill birds. Burns from hot burners and hot food in open containers.	Don't keep the bird in the kitchen, or else ventilate it regularly. Be careful, however, that there are no drafts. Do not leave hot burners or pots uncovered. Maintain wing-feather trims.
Large parrots (in an aviary)	Fighting and wounds; fatal in exceptional cases.	Never leave birds of different large species together unsupervised.
Other birds (rivals)	Fierce fighting. Development of stress; promotion of psychological illness.	Carefully introduce birds to other birds in the aviary and observe them until a pattern of dominance, which is tolerable for all birds, has evolved.
Predatory pets (dogs, cats, and ferrets)	Fighting and wounds; fatal in exceptional cases.	Never allow unknown animals in the vicinity of the birds or the aviary. If a bird's skin has been punctured by the teeth or claws of a mammal, take it immediately to an avian veterinarian for preventive antibiotic therapy.
Plate glass	Flying against it, resulting in concussion or broken neck.	Cover plate glass (windows, balcony doors, glass walls) with curtains or accustom the parrot to what is for it invisible room boundaries: lower shades to two thirds, increase the uncovered surface a bit each day. Maintain wing-feather trims.
Sharp objects (wires, nails, wood splinters)	Wounds, punctures, swallowing.	Don't leave anything lying around; be careful when building cages and attaching fencing for the aviary not to let any nails protrude.

Table of Dangers (continued)

Source of Danger	Consequences	How to Avoid
Poisons	Potentially lethal disturbances by tin, verdigris, nicotine, mercury, plastic-coated cookware, adhesives, cleaning materials, and insecticides; harmful are pencil leads, ballpoint and felt-tip pens, alcohol, coffee, avocado, and strong spices.	Remove all poisonous items from the bird's environment, or prevent it from reaching them. Be particularly careful about lead curtain weights—parrots like to gnaw on them; remove weights, if this is possible. Maintain wing-feather trims.
Poisonous trees, bushes, houseplants	Severe disturbances, often fatal.	Don't give the bird any branches of poisonous trees or bushes to gnaw. For example, the following are poisonous: acacia, yew, laburnum, viburnum, black honeysuckle, holly, dwarf elder, and many of the needle evergreens. Keep the parrot from nibbling or eating houseplants. Maintain wing-feather trims.
Smoking	Contaminated air damages delicate air sacs. Nicotine can contribute to feather picking or be fatal.	Don't smoke in the vicinity of the bird. Air the rooms regularly (avoid drafts!). Cigarettes and ashtrays should be kept out of the bird's reach.
Temperature changes	Catching cold or freezing at lower temperatures, for example, if the heat goes off.	Avoid abrupt changes of temperature as much as possible; continually check the heating system; insulate the bird house.

Showering (indoor cage): If the cockatoo has no bathing dish in its cage, it must be showered at least a couple of times weekly so that it can get rid of its feather dust. Smaller cages—without the droppings tray—may be placed, bird and all, in the bathtub and showered with a gentle spray of lukewarm water. Recently acquired birds should become accustomed to the shower slowly. Leave the cage in its usual place and carefully spray the cockatoo through the cage bars with a clean spray bottle that has never contained insecticides. In time the cockatoo will become so comfortable with this procedure that it will make happy sounds and spread its wings in anticipation at the mere sight of the spray bottle. Shower in the morning hours; this will permit the plumage to dry again by evening.

Claw Trimming: Cockatoos that are mostly kept in a cage can develop overgrown claws, despite perches with rough surfaces. The bird will have difficulty grasping, and the claws must be trimmed. To do this, take the parrot in your hand, grasp its toes between two fingers, and cut the claws with a sharp nail trimmer. Many cockatoos can be taught to submit to nail grooming without being wrapped in a towel, as veterinarians do; some will not. In addition you should smooth the cut surfaces with a nail file. Avoid the blood vessel, which extends down into the claws. In the dark cockatoo claws, the blood vessels are hard to see. For this reason, you should have expert claw cutting demonstrated by a veterinarian or professional groomer prior to your first time doing it!

Beak Trimming: Overgrowth of the horn of the beak can occur if the cockatoo doesn't have enough gnawing material available (see page 21). A metabolic disturbance resulting from an unbalanced diet can also lead to malformation of the beak, which will hinder the cockatoo's ability to eat. Only an experienced avian veterinarian or groomer should undertake beak correction.

Wing-feather Trimming: Trimming wing feathers is absolutely necessary for a cockatoo who is allowed much liberty in the home. If the bird keeps leaving its perch, it is in danger of having a number of household accidents, including drowning, being burned on a stovetop, electrocution, smashing into ceiling fans, and poisoning (see Table of Dangers, page 33). Never trim the long flight feathers too short to easily regrow, that is, shorter than the coverts (feathers that cover the base of the primaries). Never trim more than eight to ten flight feathers, counting from the outside. For most cockatoos, trimming about one half to two thirds of the length of five or six flight feathers is sufficient to safely ground them indoors. No wing trim should be trusted outdoors. Cockatoos should go outdoors only within the protection of a cage or carrier.

Cleaning the Cage and Aviary

Daily: Rinse out feed and water dishes with hot water, dry, and refill. Remove debris around the cage with the vacuum cleaner; wipe away dust, because cockatoos shed feather dust.

Weekly: Empty droppings tray twice weekly and change newspaper.

Monthly: Thoroughly scrub the cage, droppings tray, and

all the appropriate items in the cage under hot water and then dry. If you use a disinfectant, make sure it's one that is expressly for use with cage birds, possibly available through your pet dealer or veterinarian. Follow directions exactly! For some of the disinfectants, gloves are recommended. Be sure to rinse the parrot cage thoroughly and dry out well before returning the cockatoo. Watch for strong odors; they can be toxic.

Care of Aviary Birds

In contrast to the care measures of house birds, cockatoos that live in outdoor aviaries with a bird shelter need few maneuvers. Beak and claw trimming are not required as a rule, because the parrots usually have the opportunity to grind down claws and beak on the rough branches of different sizes. Beak growth is regulated naturally by gnawing natural wooden branches and nest boxes.

Showering (outdoor aviary): Although cockatoos in the outdoor aviary can bathe in a rain shower or a bath that is placed at their disposal, installation of a sprinkler system is recommended for larger aviaries. During warm summer months the system is turned on daily for a short time around midday. The plumage of the cockatoos will dry again by evening.

Small Wounds: In flight, a cockatoo often bangs against the fencing of the flight cage and so injures the sensitive skin of the nose. Also, bites on the toes acquired in fighting with rivals are not infrequent. Although sometimes such wounds bleed a great deal, it usually isn't necessary to call in the veterinarian. Rather, leave the injured bird completely at rest to give the bleeding a chance to stop. If this does not happen within a few minutes, however, apply

Stay (Mardel Laboratories, Inc.) immediately as birds have a small total blood volume. Excessive blood loss can lead quickly to stress, weakness, breathing difficulties, unconsciousness, and death.

DIET

In addition to seeds and grains, cockatoos need dark green and dark orange vegetables and fruits, along with protein supplements such as cheese or tofu, to ensure good health. Offer fresh food daily to provide your cockatoo with the opportunity to forage in the dish as it selects what it will eat.

The diet of free cockatoos is quite varied, depending on their habitat. Some cockatoo species have developed specialized diets. Those that live in the grasslands of interior Australia mainly eat small seeds, including wheat field kernels found in cultivated areas.

Cockatoos that live in the tropical rainforests are not specialized feeders, for they find quite a varied diet in their natural habitat at all seasons of the year.

Manufactured Diets

Although cockatoos in the wild can consume all manner of seed, seed is no longer considered a good basic diet for indoor cockatoos. Companion cockatoos, which can live for decades, don't fly, or forage, or find and defend nest sites. All these wild activities stimulate the bird's physique, while a companion parrot may not have nearly so many opportunities for exercise.

A companion cockatoo can easily become obese and malnourished on a mostly-seed diet.

Modern parrot diets are the product of years of scientific research and are designed with the long-lived cage bird in mind. Each bite the bird eats contains appropriately balanced nutrients while also providing necessary vitamins and minerals. My favorites are Harrison's (an organic bird diet) and Roudybush, but there are many good diets on the market. Read the labels. Look for lots of real-food ingredients rather than added chemicals.

While most modern parrot diets claim to be "complete nutrition," it is probably best to offer at least one-third of the diet in other foods.

Fruit, Green Feed, Sprouted Feed

Fruit and Vegetables: Fruits, vegetables, sprouted seeds, and cooked pasta contain important vitamins and minerals. After becoming acclimated, parrots will eat all fruits and vegetables that the store or your garden has to offer: apples, pears, plums, peaches, pomegranates, raisins, cherries, grapes, but they also do not reject exotic fruits such as oranges, bananas, mangos, papayas, or kiwis. Be sure to remove pits from apples, plums, and peaches as these can be poisonous. In addition, berry fruits of all kinds (strawberries, cranberries, blueberries, gooseberries, or red currants and mountain ash berries), as well as rose hips, are acceptable. Among the vegetables and greens, they like carrots and carrot tops, cucumbers, spinach, broccoli, celery, cooked sweet potatoes, pea pods, pumpkin, and zucchini.

Note: The fresh corn kernels full of milk that are available in the fall may be given occasionally, but corn itself is so tasty and has so little nutritional value that it should be given only as treats. The palette of suitable green feeds ranges from garden vegetables (spinach,

lettuce, or chard) to countless wild plants, such as shepherd's purse, chickweed, and dandelion. Wash all fruits and vegetables thoroughly before feeding them; they may have been sprayed with insecticides.

Sprouted Feed: In winter, when fruits and vegetables are expensive, sprouted feed can fulfill the cockatoos' vitamin and mineral requirements. Appropriate seeds are oats, wheat, and sprouted or soaked small seeds, such as those sold for parakeets. Each type of seed is sprouted separately and then combined in one dish at feeding time.

Producing Sprouted Feed: Place a two-days' supply of seeds in a dish, cover them with water, and let the seed kernels soak in a warm place for 24 hours. Then shake the swol-

Trained Owners?

It is especially important to purchase a fully weaned bird, more so for new owners of cockatoos than for any other type of parrot. Cockatoos are said to be very emotionally dependent, very code-pendent, and very manipulative. It's not unusual for severe behavioral problems to develop in cockatoos that were pur-chased unweaned. For example, breeders and parrot behavior consultants often report being asked to help finish weaning cockatoos that are well past one year old.

In one case, a Moluccan cockatoo was two years old and would not eat anything except food from a human hand when in the care of the humans who attempted to wean it. In another case, also a Moluc-can cockatoo, the bird would eat nothing except green peas, provided one at a time from the hand of the caregiver.

Both of these cases proved behavioral in origin and were related to the birds' relationships with their owners. The birds had trained the humans.

In both cases, when the birds were moved to a different home where there were different humans and other fully-weaned cockatoos, they were quite will-ing to eat independently. When they were in the homes of the novice own-ers who tried to wean them, both birds screamed incessantly and refused to eat anything provided in a bowl. It was a battle of wills that the birds always won. When the birds were placed in a cock-atoo-specific culture with humans who had different relationships with them, these charming pink giants immediately adopted the behavior of the culture.

---

len seeds in a fine-meshed sieve while rinsing thoroughly. Now spread the seeds out on a flat screen. Put them in a warm place again. During the next 24 hours, rinse the seeds thoroughly under running water several times. Depending upon the degree of warmth, the seeds will have sprouted after two or three days. They should be rinsed once more and given to the cockatoos in a separate feeding dish. Give the birds only as much as they can eat within a few hours.

Caution: Sprouted feed spoils quickly, so you must remove the leftovers within a few hours, especially in summer, and clean the dish.

Hard-shelled and tree nuts such as almonds, hazel nuts, pecans, and Brazil nuts may be given, but only as treats. Avoid peanuts, as they grow in the ground and can spread dis-eases, molds, and fungi.

Animal Protein

Although cockatoos are primarily plant-eaters, their bodies also need regular supplies of protein in small amounts. Most modern par-rot diets are formulated to provide this and are not intended to be supplemented with animal protein. However, an occasional piece of a thoroughly hard-boiled egg, a little tofu, tuna, or low-fat mozzarella cheese may be offered weekly as a treat.

Inappropriate Food

Human food, such as sausage, highly seasoned meat, french fries, or gumdrops, is not parrot food and can be very harmful to the bird. Fruit pits, including apple, can be toxic, as are avocado, caffeine, and chocolate.

Rearing Feed

During the brooding period and the raising of the young, the cockatoos should be fed the breeding or high-performance formula of your favorite diet. Supplementary soft foods can be

given. Grind up your regular parrot diet in the blender as a basis and enrich it with grated fruit, carrots, cottage cheese, feed calcium, and vitamins. Mix them all carefully until the feed has a damp, crumbly consistency.

The rearing feed should be offered to the cockatoos in a separate feeding bowl. It's possible that the parrots will accept this strange feed only after being offered it several times. Adjustment to the food already should have taken place by the time the young hatch so that there will be no interruption in feeding while the young are being raised.

Vitamins and Minerals

Vitamin preparations are unneccessary with a good-quality, modern, scientifically formulated diet. Actually, supplementing some vitamins may even be harmful. If you suspect that your bird needs vitamin or mineral supplementation, this should be determined only by an experienced avian veterinarian. For more information on important vitamins, see the table on page 44.

Drinking Water

Cockatoos need fresh tap water daily. In areas where the water quality is poor, the drinking water should be filtered or bottled water should be used. On warm summer days, change the drinking water two or three times daily.

Correct Feeding

Number of Feeding Dishes: There should be at least three feeding dishes available: one

Fat-soluble Vitamins

Vitamin	Functions	Good Sources
A	Maintenance of skin, bones, and mucous membranes; prevention of night blindness; metabolism of body cells	Egg yolk; leafy greens; yellow and orange vegetables
D_3	Essential for blood clotting; prevents egg binding; promotes absorption of calcium	Fish liver oils and egg yolk
E	Important for development of brain cells, muscles, blood, sex organs, and the embryo; increases blood circulation	Wheat germ; fruits and vegetables; chickweed; spinach; germinated seeds
K	Promotes blood clotting and liver functions	Green food; carrot tops; alfalfa; tomatoes; egg yolk; soy oil

Water-soluble Vitamins

Vitamin	Functions	Good Sources
B_1 (Thiamin)	Assists in overall growth and metabolic functions; growth of muscles and nervous system	Yeast; fruit; eggs; liver; legumes
B_2 (Riboflavin)	Development of skin, feathers, beak, and nails; egg production; metabolic functions	Eggs; green leaves; yeast; germ of good quality seeds
B_3 (Niacin)	Proper function of nervous and digestive systems; hormone production	Peanuts; whole grains; corn; liver; lean meats
B_6 (Pyridoxine)	Production of digestive juices, red blood cells, and antibodies	Bananas; peanuts; beans; whole grain cereal; egg yolk
B_{12} (Cyanocobalamin)	Essential for metabolism; assists production of red blood cells	Liver; insects; fish meal; eggs
C (Ascorbic acid)	Tissue growth; healing of wounds; red blood cell formation; promotes iron absorption	Citrus fruits and juices; leafy greens; fresh fruits; cabbage

will hold the basic diet, another drinking water, the third fruits, vegetables, or sprouted feed in rotation. At brooding, another dish is needed for rearing feed.

Note: Make sure that the dishes are always clean and that the cockatoos receive the same dishes in the usual order!

Feeding Time: Always feed at the same time, twice daily, in the morning and afternoon. Give only as much food as can be consumed in an hour and remove all but a few dry chunks of the basic diet, leaving them for a snack later.

Makeup of the Feed: The offered feed should consist of two-thirds basic diet and one-third fresh foods. Before and during the raising of young, the portion of the sprouted feed can be increased and the usual feed portion increased by the addition of rearing feed and cooked legumes (see Cockatoo Breeding, page 53).

Quantities: The size of the daily portion varies according to the size and the mobility of the cockatoos. For example, cage birds who have little opportunity for exercise need less food than larger cockatoo species and birds that live in aviaries. Don't skimp on the amount of feed, but also be careful not to overfeed.

Cleanliness and Hygiene

To prevent the spread of disease, it's important that all utensils used in feeding your cockatoo be kept very clean. They should be cleaned daily, and the empty seed hulls should be removed from the rest of the seed before refilling the containers. Many beginners make the mistake of putting fresh seed right on top of the old, hulls and all. This can lead to the lower seed never being used and becoming old, serving as a perfect breeding ground for bacteria and pests. Also, be sure not to introduce moist seeds to the feeder—these can become moldy and endanger the bird's health.

Food vessels and water containers from cages and aviaries should be also be cleaned regularly. A solution of household bleach and water makes a good disinfectant.

HEALTH AND ILLNESS

Cockatoos are normally healthy parrots, but they can occasionally become ill. Observant owners are the key to maintaining a pet bird's health. Knowing what behaviors are normal for your pet and alerting your avian veterinarian to any changes in its routine will give your pet the best chance for recovery in case of illness.

The avian veterinarian you select to care for your cockatoo will become an important partner in maintaining your bird's good health. Ideally, your cockatoo will make its first visit to the avian veterinarian on the way home from the breeder. If that is not possible, a routine examination should be performed as soon as possible to ensure your pet's health. Your cockatoo should also make an annual well-bird visit to the veterinarian to help it stay healthy. You may also take the bird to your veterinarian for wing and nail trimming.

Signs of Illness in Cockatoos

Cockatoos and other members of the parrot family are quite skilled at hiding signs of illness. However, observant bird owners soon learn what their bird's normal appearance and behavior look like. Remember that in the wild, a sick bird is often eaten by predators. Your pet cockatoo has not lost this natural ability to conceal illness.

Review the signs of illness listed below. Contact your avian veterinarian's office for an appointment if your pet's appearance, activity level, appetite, or behavior changes.

- Fluffed feathers
- Loss of interest in surroundings
- No vocalizations
- Drooping wings
- Lameness
- Appetite loss
- Weight loss
- Excessive sleeping
- Changes in elimination pattern
- Changes in droppings
- Breathing problems
- Runny nares (nostrils) or eyes

First Aid

Although having your cockatoo treated by an avian veterinarian is always best, certain situations will require some first aid measures from you. The following describes some common injuries and accidents that your bird may encounter and some steps you can take to help your bird before it arrives at your veterinarian's office or animal emergency room.

Remember that these treatment suggestions do not replace veterinary care. Follow your veterinarian's advice and treatment recommendations at all times. Your veterinarian has the advantage of knowing your cockatoo's medical history. He or she is knowledgeable and experienced about the best treatments to pursue in emergency situations.

Bleeding: Apply direct pressure or place a pinch of cornstarch on the wound to stop bleeding. If your cockatoo has a chewed or broken blood feather, pull the remaining feather out with needle-nose pliers. Then apply direct pressure and cornstarch to the feather follicle.

Breathing Problems: Run a warm, steamy shower to create a humid environment. Then place the bird into its cage in the room.

Broken Bones: Keep the bird warm and quiet. Splint the broken bone only if your veterinarian recommends it.

Burns: Spray cool water over the burned skin. Do not use butter or other greasy ointments.

Frostbite: Bring the bird indoors. Keep it warm and quiet.

Head Injury/Concussion: Protect your bird from additional injury, and monitor activity. Keep your bird warm and quiet.

Heatstroke: Place the bird in front of a fan or in a bowl of cool water to lower its temperature. Provide cool water for it to drink, or give your bird water using an eyedropper.

Lead Poisoning: A cockatoo's curiosity may cause it to consume a household item that contains lead, such as a drapery weight, which could lead to lead poisoning. Signs of this condition include blindness, depression, weakness, or walking in circles. Successful treatment requires quick action, and the treatment could take several weeks to complete.

Poisoning: In addition to lead poisoning, cockatoos can come in contact with other household poisons that may harm them. Signs of poisoning include diarrhea, regurgitation, bloody droppings, convulsions, or paralysis. Quick action is required to treat a poisoned parrot successfully. So contact an avian veterinarian immediately.

Seizures: Place the bird into a smaller cage, such as a travel carrier, to prevent additional injuries. Keep it quiet and warm.

Shock: Keep your pet warm and quiet.

An Avian First Aid Kit

Having a few basic supplies on hand can make facing a veterinary emergency a little easier. Include the following items in your cockatoo's first aid kit:

- Bandages
- Cornstarch or styptic powder to control bleeding
- Disinfectant solution
- Energy supplement, such as Gatorade
- Eyedropper
- Grooming tools (nail clippers, nail file, needle-nose pliers)
- Heating pad or other heat source
- Saline solution
- Scissors with rounded tips
- Small flashlight
- Towels for catching and holding your bird
- Tweezers

Seek Professional Help

If your bird suffers an injury or becomes ill, take it to your avian veterinarian. First aid measures help stabilize your pet, but they do not usually provide complete care to resolve the problem.

Time is of the essence when dealing with a sick parrot. As noted earlier, parrots can be masters at hiding signs of illness. By the time you notice your pet is not acting right, it may already be critically ill.

Common Cockatoo Illnesses

Although cockatoos are typically healthy birds, they can still contract certain avian diseases. If your bird shows signs of illness, take it to an avian veterinarian for treatment. Trying to treat a sick parrot with over-the-counter medication wastes time and money. Diagnostic tests are required to determine the cause of the bird's illness. These can be conducted only by a veterinarian, who can then prescribe a

course of treatment. The following lists the most common avian illnesses your cockatoo can contract.

Aspergillosis: Aspergillosis is named for the fungus, *Aspergillis*, that causes it. This disease invades a cockatoo's respiratory system and makes it difficult for the bird to breathe. Healthy birds are less likely to contract aspergillosis than are birds with other health problems. Antifungal medications can treat this disease. However, preventing it is easier by keeping the bird's cage and environment clean.

Candidiasis: This disease is caused by a yeast, *Candida albicans*. Healthy adult birds are less likely to catch candidiasis than are young birds that are being hand-fed or birds that are recovering from another illness. Signs of this illness include white, cheesy growths in the mouth along with appetite loss. Affected birds will have difficulty emptying their crops, and they will regurgitate often. Antifungal drugs are used to treat candidiasis. The disease can be prevented by feeding a diet containing high levels of vitamin A.

Egg Binding: When a female bird cannot lay an egg, she is egg bound. She will strain in an attempt to expel the egg but may require surgery to remove it safely. If your bird sits, panting on the cage floor, and unable to stand or move, she may be egg bound. Heat and humidity such as that created by a hot shower in a closed bathroom may help the bird pass the egg. Contact an avian veterinarian for additional instructions on helping an egg-bound hen.

Giardia: Like aspergillosis and candidiasis, *Giardia* takes its name from the protozoan, *Giardia psittaci*, that causes it. Although this disease can be difficult to detect, cockatoos that lose weight, pass loose droppings or begin feather picking should be tested. Other signs of the disease include appetite loss and depression. Medication from an avian veterinarian can treat *Giardia*.

Obesity: Obesity causes certain problems, and also creates the potential for other long-term health issues in pet birds. Sometimes the causative agent is a poorly functioning thyroid. In most cases, though, an obese bird eats more calories than it uses during its daily activities. Some cockatoos can be prone to obesity. Feed a balanced diet with low levels of fats to prevent your bird from becoming overweight.

Invest in a gram scale, monitor the bird's weight, and also offer ample opportunities for out-of-cage exercise, such as a play gym or climbing tree.

Polyomavirus: Originally known as French molt, polyomavirus affects a bird's tail and flight feathers. The feathers may not develop in some birds, while other birds have poorly formed feathers. Birds contract polyomavirus through contact with affected birds or with the feather dust or droppings from a sick bird. Signs of infection include weakness, appetite loss, diarrhea, paralysis, regurgitation, and bleeding beneath the skin. Although this disease has no cure, vaccine is available to prevent it.

Proventricular Dilatation Disease (PDD): First discovered in macaws, PDD is a serious digestive disorder. Originally known as macaw wasting disease, it was first thought to affect only those avian species. It is now known to affect many pet bird species, including cockatoos. Affected birds may pass whole seeds in their droppings. Other signs of this fatal illness include seizures, regurgitation, and depression.

Psittacine Circovirus 1: Formerly known as psittacine beak and feather disease syndrome or PBFDS, this fatal viral disease was once thought to be a cockatoo-specific problem. The main sign of psittacine circovirus 1 is pinched or clubbed feathers. Affected birds can also have beak fractures and mouth ulcers. Psittacine circovirus 1 is highly contagious. It most often affects birds under the age of three years.

Psittacosis: Some parrots carry psittacosis their entire lives. These carrier birds may never show signs of illness, but they may infect both pets and people. Affected birds may have appetite and weight loss, depression, and unusual lime-green droppings. Antibiotic treatments clear up the infection in both parrots and people.

Vitamin A Deficiency: Vitamin A is a vital nutrient in keeping a pet bird's immune system healthy. However, birds that eat a seed-only diet are at risk of suffering from a deficiency of this important vitamin. Signs of a vitamin A deficiency include mouth sores, vision problems, breathing difficulties, and chronic infections. Feeding a diet that includes a variety of vegetables and fruits rich in vitamin A is the best prevention against this problem.

Upper Respiratory Infections: Upper respiratory infections used to be common in birds that ate primarily seed-based diets, but any pet bird can develop such an infection. Signs of illness include tail bobbing, breathing difficulties, fluffed feathers, and discharge from the bird's nares (nostrils) and eyes. Antibiotics prescribed by an avian veterinarian can usually clear up these infections.

COCKATOO BREEDING

Successful cockatoo breeding is the only legal way for future pet owners to have cockatoos to enjoy. Cockatoos have not been exported in large numbers since the early 1990s, so captive-bred birds are the future for the pet industry.

Captive-bred birds make better pets because they are accustomed to people from day one. They are healthier than the wild-caught birds that previously found their way into pet homes. Despite the need for captive-bred cockatoos, the process of breeding these birds is a time-consuming task that requires a certain set of skills. Novice cockatoo owners may not be equipped to devote the time, energy, and money required to breed baby cockatoos successfully. So it is a job best left to the experts. Take time to learn all that you can about a particular cockatoo species before attempting to breed birds. Befriend breeders who raise the species you are interested in, and shadow them as they raise a clutch of chicks.

Species Protection

Captive breeding of cockatoos helps preserve different species for the future. Along with other species that are native to the islands of the South Pacific, cockatoos are endangered or threatened with extinction. The cause of this is the ongoing destruction of their habitat. Expanses of forest are being recklessly destroyed in order to gain usable land area. With them, the breeding and sleeping trees of many cockatoo species are falling victim to the power saw. Successful conservation can be achieved only with the combination of species protection by law and purposeful cockatoo breeding by zoos and fanciers.

Controlling International Trade

All 21 species of cockatoo are protected under an international agreement called the Convention on International Trade in Endangered Species of Wild Fauna and Flora, which is CITES for short. The groundwork for CITES was laid in 1963, with 80 member countries signing the original agreement 10 years later. Today, 175 nations have signed the agreement, which makes importing, exporting, or trading endangered wildlife illegal.

CITES has three appendices. Appendix I lists animals that are threatened with extinction. Appendix II lists endangered animals. Appendix III lists animals that a member country has requested be considered for protection.

Five species of cockatoos—the Goffin's cockatoo (*Cacatua goffiniana*), the Red-vented cockatoo (*Cacatua haematuropygia*), the Moluccan cockatoo (*Cacatua moluccensis*), the Sulphur-crested cockatoo (*Cacatua sulphurea*), and the Palm cockatoo (*Probosciger aterrimus*) are listed on Appendix I of CITES. The 16 remaining species are listed on Appendix II.

Successful Breeding

No matter what species of cockatoo you are breeding, you must follow a few basic steps regarding housing and diet to improve breeding success.

Prerequisites

Before you begin breeding cockatoos, make sure you have the following items on hand. Have everything ready before the nesting cycle begins.

Housing: A cockatoo pair in a bird room or in an outdoor aviary, rather than in a high-traffic family room, offers the best conditions for successful breeding. Pairs should be somewhat removed from family comings and goings and from traffic noise. If you have a system of several aviaries together, you must make sure that the breeding pair is not disturbed by neighbor birds during their courtship preparations. Erect screens if necessary.

Additions to the Diet: If cockatoos eat a balanced, varied diet, nutrient supplements before and during breeding are usually unnec-

essary. Nevertheless, breeders should maintain a certain seasonal rhythm in the feed composition for breeding birds. The diet should give the birds a sense of harvest time, because wild birds reproduce in a cycle designed to feed babies when food supplies are greatest.

Nest Boxes: Used for breeding these should have a square base and can be obtained from a pet store or made at home. You should reinforce the edges of the entry hole with strips of tin to prevent the cockatoos from expanding the entry hole with their beaks. You should also install wire fencing or other sturdy wire underneath the entrance hole inside the box so the breeding birds will have a climbing aid.

Litter: Nest boxes or hollow trees should be lined with a layer of wood humus about 4 inches (10 cm) thick, which should be slightly dampened shortly before the time of nesting. Slightly damp litter will allow the eggs to settle properly under the weight of the female.

Mounting Nest Boxes: You should mount the nest boxes under the roof of the aviary or the bird shelter. If possible, place the boxes so they can be easily checked without disturbing the nesting parent birds.

Note: Cockatoos nest only at the time of brooding. After brooding, remove all nest boxes. Clean, disinfect, and repair them. Store the boxes until the next nesting cycle.

Pairing

Even if you have a known male and female (see Determining Gender, page 15), establishing a harmonious pair is not easy. All birds intended for breeding should belong to the same species or subspecies. Grown birds can become used to each other with difficulty (see Getting Used to Each Other, page 30). On the

other hand, if several young birds of different genders live together in one aviary, harmonious cockatoo pair bonds usually develop quickly and spontaneously.

Sometimes spontaneous pairing occurs in adult birds as it does with young birds. However, two cockatoos may never adjust to each other, even after several attempts. In extreme cases, the male bird will injure or even kill an incompatible female bird. So carefully monitor all introductions for the birds' safety.

Brooding Period

With cockatoos kept in an indoor aviary or in a bird room, the brooding period can occur at any season. If the parrots live in an outdoor aviary and winter over in the bird shelter,

the brooding birds will eventually establish a seasonal rhythm. Brooding season begins about the end of April. Egg laying occurs at the beginning of May, and hatching of young occurs at the beginning of June. Young birds leave the nest from the middle of July to the beginning of August, with stragglers leaving somewhat later. Molting occurs in September and October. After that, the cockatoos go into a winter rest period until the next spring.

Courtship and Mating

In many cockatoo species, the courtship display is very impressive.

Display Behavior: With spread feathers and wings, fanned tail, and erect crest feathers, the male woos the female. This so-called display

behavior serves both to scare off rival suitors and to court the female.

Mutual Preening: Another courtship behavior often seen is mutual preening, which is the mutual "scratching" of two birds. This behavior strengthens pair bonding. Both birds can enjoy preening on places like the head or rump area that a single bird can reach by itself only with difficulty.

Copulation: Courtship usually leads to mating. The male mounts the female so that their cloacas (into which both the spermatic duct and the oviduct empty) are joined. Shortly before egg laying, the readiness to mate and the frequency of copulation increases.

Egg Laying and Brooding

The end of the courtship period is followed by egg laying. At intervals of two to three days—in the afternoon or early morning—the cockatoo female lays two to three uniformly white, round-oval eggs. In the species described in this book, the female and male take turns brooding, although the greater part of it falls to the female. Both parents can get food independently of each other from time to time. For this reason, cockatoos lack the partner-feeding behavior noted in other parrots, a social pattern in which the male provides the female and the young with food during the brooding and raising periods.

The length of the brooding period varies, depending on the species. However, the length is usually somewhere between 25 and 30 days. See the chapter Cockatoo Species, beginning on page 69, for more details.

Development of the Young

Young cockatoos hatch at the same interval at which the eggs were laid. At birth they

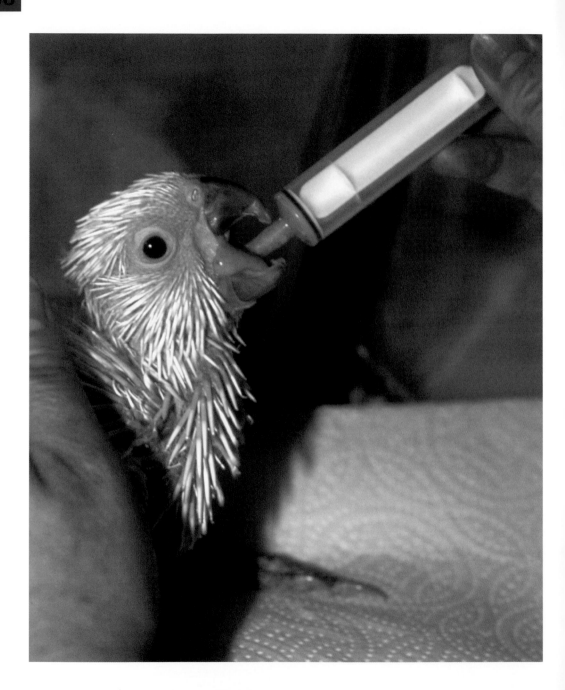

are—like all altricial birds—naked, blind, and completely helpless. Their bodily development takes a fairly long time. They open their eyes after only several weeks, and a thick coat of down develops to protect them from the cold. Between 60 and 100 days—depending on the species—the young cockatoos get their complete plumage and can leave the nest. Before they are completely independent, however, they are cared for and fed by their parents for another two to three weeks.

Note: Cockatoos as a rule raise only one young bird out of a two- or three-egg clutch. The remaining one or two eggs are a reserve, so to speak, in case something goes wrong with the oldest nestling in the first two or three days. If the first bird to hatch develops normally, the feeding and care of the younger animals is sometimes neglected. These younger ones often pine away or die prematurely. If hatchlings are being neglected, you can try to raise the younger birds by hand.

Hand Raising

Hand raising may be necessary when adult cockatoos leave their eggs because of frequent disturbance or because they cannot give enough care to all the young. If you notice this soon enough, take the eggs from the nest and continue developing them in an incubator. Young birds hatched in an incubator, or nestlings that have been neglected by their parents, may be raised by hand.

Housing: Keep the parrot chicks at a temperature of about 97°F (36°C). An infrared lamp is very good for this. Choose a container for keeping the nestling that is not too large. For instance, you can use a hospital cage or a wooden box with a glass front. The quarters should be controlled thermostatically. The temperature should be reduced gradually as the birds mature.

Food and Feeding: At the very beginning, neonatal cockatoos should receive a quality hand-feeding formula, preferably the same brand you have been feeding the parents, every two hours between 6 A.M. and 12 P.M. Offer only fresh food at every feeding. Its temperature should be 104 to 105.8°F (40–41°C) at feeding. In the beginning it can be administered with a large-volume plastic eyedropper. Later you can use a teaspoon if the sides have been bent inward. With increasing age, feed the young birds only every three to four hours. As the birds near weaning, add other foods and offer them lukewarm or even at room temperature.

It is difficult to manage the crossover to eating independently, and this step can be frustrating for inexperienced breeders. Get the young cockatoos used to it step by step. At first, give them the familiar formula in the feeding dish. Later offer them soft fruit and greenery. Finally offer diet pellets, first broken up and then whole. Young cockatoos accomplish eating independently most easily by watching neighboring older birds. Be careful to see that the young birds are never subject to sudden temperature changes or drafts. Only when they are fully feathered should cockatoo young be kept at room temperature without any additional heat source.

UNDERSTANDING COCKATOOS

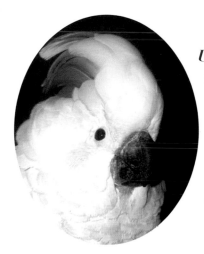

Understanding cockatoo behavior is one of the most important things an owner can do. Cockatoos require a lot of attention from their owners, and some birds can become quite needy. If not managed properly, this neediness can turn into problem behaviors, such as biting, screaming, or feather picking.

How Cockatoos Live Together in Nature

Quite a bit is known about the way of life and the behavior of cockatoos in their natural habitat—in contrast to most of the other parrot species.

Group Size

The cockatoo species described in this book live together in flocks except during the brooding period. Such flocks consist of single animals, pairs, and families that gather at common eating, drinking, and sleeping places. While searching for food, cockatoos—particularly those of the plains and desert habitats—congregate in large groups. Often one will encounter groups of several thousand birds at favorite spots. In contrast, groups of those species that are found in the tropical rain forests outside the Australian continent are much smaller, containing only 8 to 10 birds.

The Communal Life

Gathering into groups primarily ensures that cockatoos will find food. Meeting social needs cannot be assumed to be an important function because the birds and the group do not usually enter into any closer social bonds—except for the choice of mate. Rather, the communal life can be characterized as a kind of open association in which the individual animals don't necessarily know each other and there is no firmly defined order of dominance.

The advantage of a federation is that feeding places can be better scouted and can be secured against rival feeders. Of course there are also frequent quarrels within the cockatoo flock about the best feeding places, sleeping places, and nest holes.

Expected Behaviors in Companion Cockatoos

You can expect your companion cockatoo to exhibit the following behaviors.

Eating and Drinking

The cockatoo removes the outer coverings of seeds, fruits, and vegetables in its beak with its tongue. Like most large parrots, the cockatoo uses its foot like a hand, to hold morsels of food and lift food to its beak. To drink, the bird scoops up water with its lower beak and tips its head back to swallow.

Resting and Sleeping

Healthy birds rest and sleep on one leg; the other leg is drawn up into the feathers. The body plumage may be fluffed slightly. The head is usually turned back and into the back feathers to the base of the beak. The eyes may be closed either completely or partially.

Exercise

Cockatoos that live in captivity are in nearly constant motion all day long. In the cage, they climb and do gymnastics tirelessly. If they are in an outdoor aviary, you will find them almost constantly climbing, scratching, gnawing, or flying. Besides their natural motions, cockatoos are also able to mimic playful movements with training. Cockatoos are especially famous for their dexterity. They can carry things, push little toy cars, eat from a spoon, and much more.

Running and Hopping: Cockatoos, especially those of the dry plains and grasslands of interior Australia, are "good on their feet." They find their food predominantly on the ground. These birds can also be observed frequently running in the aviary or cage. The cockatoo's body is held erect as it runs with long, stiff-gaited steps. Likewise, hopping is accompanied by an erect body and crest.

Scratching: Some cockatoo species love to scratch in the dirt, on the floor, or in fabric corners, such as in a sofa or overstuffed chair. This behavior has developed because they find their food mainly on the ground. The most noticeable adaptation to this form of food seeking is seen in slender-built cockatoos, which have elongated upper beaks suitable for digging.

Climbing: Most cockatoo species possess excellent climbing ability. Therefore, you should offer your cockatoo plenty of things to climb in a cage and in the aviary.

Flying: In their natural habitat, many cockatoo species often cover long distances in their search for feeding places. They are excellent flyers. In captivity, a cockatoo must be trained and encouraged to flap a couple of times daily until it is winded. This exercise stimulates the bird's metabolism and can be a primary defense in the prevention of feather picking and excessive screaming.

Showers: Wild cockatoos sometimes fly, forage, and reproduce in blinding rain. In captivity, showering can function like exercise to help the wing feather–trimmed birds vent nervous energy that might come out as unwanted

attention-demanding or feather-damaging behaviors.

Comfort Behaviors

Comfort behaviors include patterns concerned with the body care of the cockatoo.

Preening: A cockatoo preens its plumage several times daily by drawing the individual feathers through its beak. The bird usually begins with the smaller feathers and then polishes the primaries, secondaries, and tail feathers. Finally, by means of rubbing movements with the head and beak, the bird distributes the feather dust over its plumage.

Head Scratching: Also part of plumage care, the bird lifts its foot to its head and scratches while turning and twisting its head.

Some cockatoos occasionally use little branches to help scratch. An unusual behavior is the hesitant, almost slow-motion head scratching that looks rather like the bird is swimming the crawl. This behavior is primarily seen in single birds—perhaps satisfying their need for mutual preening with a partner bird in this way.

Beak Care: The cockatoo removes dirt and food particles from its beak by rubbing it on a hard surface, such as the perch. Cockatoos also grind their beaks, sometimes quite noisily, as they fall asleep. Beak grinding is an absolutely normal and frequently observed comfort behavior.

Showering: All cockatoos love to take showers when they get used to the procedure. They spread their wings slightly and fan their tails. During the shower, they twist and turn their whole body and flap their wings so that the feathers get damp all over.

Stretching: Cockatoos frequently stretch and yawn after rest periods. The wing and leg on the same side of the body will be stretched to the rear/down. At the same time, the corresponding side of the tail will be spread. Sometimes you will also see the bird lifting both wings over its back and spreading them. Yawning stretches the beak parts, although this primarily serves to supply the body with oxygen.

Managing Behavior in Companion Cockatoos

Young cockatoos come with great cooperation skills. Therefore, step-up practice and peek-a-boos with a towel need to be performed only minimally (a minute or two a couple of times a week) in order teach and maintain cooperation skills. On the other hand, hand-fed domestic cockatoos may fail to develop emotional and behavioral independence.

Special care must be taken starting starting from the newly weaned baby's first days in your home to encourage the development of curiosity and independent play. The bird should not be let near anything that holds sentimental value for you. It might rip, shred, chew, or otherwise dismantle it to its heart's content. Provide the bird with many different toys of many different types and textures. Set a good example for the bird by demonstrating independent activities such as reading, working on the computer, or washing dishes.

Although a young cockatoo has a need to be cuddled and snuggled, constant snuggling can become addictive to the bird, who may wish to do absolutely nothing except cuddle and preen. This can lead to some problem behaviors, which are outlined below.

Behaviors That Indicate a Problem

Cockatoos can be prone to three significant behavior problems: biting, screaming, and feather picking. Any or all of these behaviors can develop if a bird feels neglected by its owner. This is why you must teach the

Step-up Practice

From its first days in the home, a well-socialized, newly weaned baby cockatoo expects lots of cuddling. The juvenile bird also needs to learn more than just cuddling. A young cockatoo learns (or rather, is conditioned) to cooperate in social settings when it engages in interactive activities with people. Step-up practice is the most common of these exercises. The routine, when practiced almost daily, needs to be no more than a few minutes in duration. This interactive practice works best when it includes the following five features.

1. Practice stepping the bird from the hand to and from an unfamiliar perch.

2. Practice stepping the bird from hand to hand.

3. Practice stepping the bird from a hand-held perch to and from an unfamiliar perch.

4. Practice stepping the bird from a hand-held perch to a handheld perch.

5. Practice stepping the bird from a familiar perch to and from both hands and to and from handheld perches.

Unless the bird is cooperative and well-patterned enough to step up from an unfamiliar perch in unfamiliar territory, it may refuse to step up from the cage or other familiar perch. In an older or unsocialized cockatoo, step-up practice might initially have to take place outside the bird's established territory in the home. A laundry room or hallway is usually perfect, as the bird will probably never spend much time in these areas and therefore should not develop territorial behavior in them. A cooperative bird can be successfully patterned to this exercise anywhere.

Be sure to offer affection and praise after each completed step up. Always discontinue step-up practice only after the bird successfully completes the command. This is crucial to good patterning. If the command is unsuccessful, alter technique, approach, or prompting mannerisms rather than continue with unsuccessful methods. Be careful not to reinforce unsuccessful patterns. Even if the bird must be placed onto the floor to achieve a successful step-up command, unless the bird is having a panic reaction, do not return it to its territory until just after a successful cooperative interaction.

There is no substitute for warm, genuine human enthusiasm as a reward for the bird's success in stepping up. Especially with shy or cautious cockatoos, the most important part of this exercise is the bird's enjoyment of the process. If the bird is not eagerly cooperating with step ups and step-up practice, something is going wrong. Call in an experienced parrot behavior consultant as quickly as possible.

cockatoo to entertain itself from its first days in your home.

Biting

Biting can be a dangerous behavior in a cockatoo because its strong beak can leave a deep wound or even break bones. Biting is not a natural parrot behavior but is one that captive birds learn when trying to control their environment.

To prevent your bird from biting, provide a variety of chew toys, a varied diet, and regular out-of-cage exercise opportunities. Monitor your behavior around the cockatoo, especially when offering a hand as a perch. Do not pull away as the bird reaches for your hand with its beak; this is how it tests the strength of a new perch. Do not tease the bird by holding toys or treats just out of its reach or pulling them away immediately after offering them.

Screaming

Cockatoos will vocalize frequently during the day. A normal cockatoo routine calls for making noise at dawn and at sunrise, as well as vocalizing throughout the day.

Some cockatoos take this vocalizing too far and become screamers. A cockatoo's scream is not a sound to be taken lightly. So redirect the bird to a different behavior. To change the screaming behavior, though, you will first have to determine the cause behind it.

Reassurance: Some cockatoos begin screaming to seek reassurance from their owners because they are lonely or they may feel as if they are not part of the family. A quiet verbal reassurance such as, "I'm here. Are you all right?" can help settle the cockatoo. In other cases, you may need to check on the bird without immediately letting it out of the cage for one-on-one time with you. Reassure the bird that all is well and return to what you were doing. This verbal reassurance also works well if the cockatoo appears to have been frightened by a loud noise or a strange person in the home.

Enjoyment: If your cockatoo seems to enjoy screaming, you can redirect the energy into whistling or talking instead. When the bird screams, whistle back at it or say a word you want it to learn. Lavish attention on the bird if it mimics your behavior, and ignore it if it continues to scream. In time, the cockatoo will likely talk or whistle instead of scream to get your attention.

Feather Picking

Cockatoos can be especially prone to feather picking, which can quickly become compulsive if it's left untreated. Although it looks painful to us, the act of picking calms some birds.

If you notice that your bird suddenly starts pulling his feathers out, contact your avian veterinarian for an evaluation. Sometimes feather pulling has a physical cause, such as an infestation with a parasite called *Giardia*. In other cases, stress, boredom, insecurity, breeding frustration, or nervousness may be to blame.

To prevent feather picking from becoming a habit, offer your cockatoo a varied diet that includes chances to play with its food, including peas in the pod, pomegranate slices, corn on the cob, and nuts in the shell. Also provide a variety of toys, and replace worn or frayed toys as soon as possible. Provide regular out-of-cage playtimes for your bird, too.

COCKATOO SPECIES

Cockatoos are native to Australia, New Guinea and some islands of the South Pacific. Of the 21 cockatoo species found in nature, only about six are commonly kept as pets. Cockatoo lovers may have an opportunity to see rarer species at zoos or aviaries around the country.

Interesting Facts About Cockatoos

Parrots constitute some 320 to 330 of the approximately 8,600 bird species on the earth. In the order of parrots there are 18 cockatoo species, including the cockatiels.

Like the majority of parrots, cockatoos have a powerful, mobile curved beak and a zygo-dactyl toe formation (four toes, two front opposing two back). Their mostly white or dark plumage, their expressive facial fans, and their long, movable forehead and crown feathers (recumbent and recurve) distinguish them visually from the other parrots.

Distribution: Cockatoos are distributed over wide areas of Australia and Indonesia. The Philippine cockatoo has the northernmost distribution area. It inhabits the Philippine island of Luzon (north latitude). The Funereal cockatoo and the Greater Sulphur-crested cockatoo have the southernmost ranges. Both species,

along with others, are found on Tasmania. Cockatoos inhabit three environments: tropical rain forests with high temperatures and heavy rainfall; grassy plains as transition zones between rain forests and desert (humid and dry savannas); and wastes with prairie-like vegetation and scant, irregular rainfall.

Cockatoo Species: The species described in this book are indicated with an asterisk.

Family: *Cacatuidae*—cockatoos

Subfamily: *Cacatuinae*—true cockatoos

Genus: *Probosciger*

Species: Palm cockatoo (*P. aterrimus*, five subspecies)

Genus: *Calyptoihynchus*

Species: Red-tailed black or Banksian cockatoo (*C. magnificus*, four subspecies)

Glossy black cockatoo (*C. lathami*)

Funereal or Yellow-tailed black cockatoo (*C. funereus*, three subspecies)

White-tailed black or Baudin's black cockatoo (*C. baudinii*, four subspecies)

Genus: *Callocephalon*
Species: Gang-gang or red-crowned or helmeted cockatoo (*C. fimbriatum*)
Genus: *Eolophus*
Species: Rose-breasted or Roseate cockatoo, galah* (*E. roseicapillus*, three subspecies)
Genus: *Cacatua*
Species: Philippine or red-vented cockatoo (*C. haematuropygia*)
Goffin's cockatoo* (*C. goffini*)
Bare-eyed cockatoo or Little Corella (*C. sanguinea*, two subspecies)
Slender-billed cockatoo (*C. tenuirostris*, two subspecies)
Ducorp's cockatoo (*C. ducorps*)
Blue-eyed cockatoo (*C. ophthalmica*)
Greater Sulphur-crested cockatoo* (*C. galerita*, four subspecies)

Lesser Sulphur-crested cockatoo* (*C. sulphurea*, six subspecies)
Umbrella-crested, White-crested, or Greater White-crested cockatoo* (*C. alba*)
Moluccan cockatoo* (*C. moluccensis*)
Leadbeater's cockatoo (*C. leadbeateri*, four subspecies)

Frequently Kept Cockatoo Species

Altogether, there are only six cockatoo species that are usually available commercially. A detailed description of each of these species follows.

Rose-breasted or Roseate Cockatoo, or Galah

Eolophus roseicapillus (3 subspecies)
Description: Total length 13½ inches (35 cm). Male: upper side gray, underside rose-red; forehead, crown, neck, and (recumbent) crest feathers pale pink, almost white; undertail coverts gray; tail underside gray-black; beak yellowish gray; legs gray; iris dark brown to black. Female: similar to male but iris red to red-brown.

Distribution: Entire interior of Australian continent.

Habitat: Primarily dry areas, but also other forms of climate and vegetation; frequently in the vicinity of artificially-created water areas, in parks and gardens.

Maintenance: Because they have been traditionally among the most expensive parrots, rosies were usually kept as breeders. They are skillful fliers, even indoors. As aviary birds they are relatively undemanding and exceptionally climate-resistant.

Breeding: In courtship the male struts up to the female, bows his head forward, and raises his crest. A brief chattering of the beak accompanies wooing. Before egg laying the females line the nest box with small branches and leaves. The clutch consists of three to four eggs, which are brooded by both parents taking turns for 25 days. After about seven weeks the young leave the nest box.

As Companions: Cautious to the point of sometimes being shy. Clear and distinct human mimicks. Rosies have a reputation for both gnawing less and screaming less loudly than other common companion cockatoos. Typically high energy, but occasionally tending to obesity.

Goffin's Cockatoo
Cacatua goffini

Description: Total length 12½ inches (32 cm). Male: basic plumage color white; bridle pink; small recumbent crest; undersides of wing and tail yellowish; unfeathered eye ring gray-white; beak whitish yellow; legs light gray; iris black. Female: similar to male except iris brown-red.

Distribution: Exclusively on Tanimbar Island off New Guinea.

Habitat: Primarily forest.

Maintenance: One of the smallest cockatoos, it appears not to be very popular among parrot fanciers; very little has been reported about it over the last ten years. Goffin's cockatoos offer no problems in maintenance and are undemanding. They can be wintered over in a dry, draft-free, slightly heated bird house. Nevertheless, Goffin's cockatoos have a strong need to gnaw and a relatively loud voice.

Breeding: The first successful German attempt was made in 1978 by Th. Weise in

Dortmund. These little cockatoos display rather inconspicuous courtship behavior, which is accompanied (in both sexes) by chattering of the beak. The clutch consists of two to three eggs. The brooding period runs 26 to 28 days. It is not known exactly when the young leave the nest box. Accounts on record range from 60 to 85 days.

As Companions: A cautious, reactionary bird with a tendency to form extreme and unpredictable bonds that can foster unwanted behaviors, such as feather plucking. Often scream, even in the dark. Like other types of companion cockatoos, Goffin's cockatoos allowed to roam on the floor can easily develop a habit of attacking toes.

Greater Sulphur-crested Cockatoo
Cacatua galerita (4 subspecies)

Description: Total length 19½ inches (50 cm). Male: basic plumage color white; ear spots—depending on subspecies—pale yellow to yellow; recurve crest, undersides of tail and wings yellow; unfeathered eye ring white; beak gray-black; legs gray; iris deep dark brown to black. Female: similar to male, but iris is reddish brown. The triton cockatoo (*C. galerita triton*) differs from all the other subspecies in that it has a blue, unfeathered eye ring.

Distribution: Northeastern and southern Australia, Tasmania, King Island, New Guinea, Aru Island.

Habitat: Open forested land, usually in the vicinity of water courses; occasionally also swampy areas and tropical rain forests.

Maintenance: After the Moluccan cockatoo, the Greater Sulphur-crested cockatoo is the largest of the common cockatoos. It has an outstanding need to gnaw and utters piercing screams. Aviary birds are robust and unde-

manding. Except in the coldest of climates, they can even be wintered in unheated, but dry and draft-free, quarters.

Breeding: Greater Sulphur-crested cockatoos exhibit impressive courtship behavior, with fanned tail feathers, erected crests, and jerky display movements. The clutch consists of two to three eggs. The brooding time lasts around 30 days (both sexes take turns brooding, during the day by the male and at night by the female). The nestling period lasts around 85 days. Young birds feed independently in about 100 days.

As Companions: Famous screamers and chewers, the Greater Sulphur-crested cockatoos are often unsuited to apartments or other closely spaced dwellings.

Lesser Sulphur-crested Cockatoo
Cacatua sulphurea (6 subspecies)

Description: Total length 13¼ inches (34 cm). Male: basic plumage color white; round ear spots, recurve crest, undersides of wings, and tail yellow. Female: similar to male but iris turns brownish red after the third year. Of all six subspecies of the Lesser Sulphur-crested cockatoo, the Citron-crested cockatoo (*C. sulphurea citrinocristata*) is the most striking. Instead of the yellow markings it has orange ear spots and an orangey crest.

Distribution: Celebes (Sulawesi), Sunda Islands, several small islands of the Flores and the Java Seas.

Habitat: Open forest areas, occasionally unbroken forests and wheat-growing areas.

Maintenance: Most frequently kept in captivity of any of the cockatoo species; at one time they were particularly preferred as house pets, but today they are increasingly kept as pairs in the aviary. Lesser Sulphur-crested cockatoos need roomy quarters, for they are good fliers; they are more active than the Greater Sulphur-crested. Their tremendous beak strength requires a sturdily built aviary. Natural branches and little boards should be provided regularly to prevent boredom and to satsify their need to gnaw.

Breeding: Easiest to breed of all the cockatoos. Choosing mates sometimes turns out to be difficult, however, for it can happen that the male will be very aggressive toward the female and chase her through the aviary, often to the point of exhaustion, and also drive her away from the feeding place. It is wise, therefore, to provide escape possibilities and blinders for the protection of the female. Sometimes it will be necessary to change

mates. The courtship is very impressive, with erected crest, spread tail, erect strutting, and jerky bowing, similar to that of the Greater Sulphur-crested cockatoo. The clutch consists of two to three eggs, which are brooded by both sexes. Brooding lasts about 24 days (in Citron-crested cockatoos 27 to 28 days). The nestling period takes eight to ten weeks. Young do not acquire the black beak until they are approximately seven months old.

As Companions: Famous screamers and chewers, even the smallest Lesser Sulphur-crested cockatoos may be unsuited to apartments. Mature males may be especially unpredictable biters.

Umbrella, White-crested, or Greater White-crested Cockatoo
Cacatua alba

Description: Total length 17½ inches (45 cm). Male: basic plumage color white; broad recurve crest white; unfeathered eye ring cream white; beak black; legs dark gray; iris dark brown to black. Female: similar to male, but iris red-brown.

Distribution: Moluccas Obi, Batjan, Soa-Siu (Tidore), and Ternate.

Habitat: Largely unknown; some authorities believe that the birds live in forests and around farmland in pairs or small groups.

Maintenance: Umbrella pairs must be kept only in roomy, sturdy quarters, for they are very loud and their beaks are strong enough to destroy everything. Aviary keeping is recommended, however; there the birds are relatively undemanding, but they do need a slightly warmed house for protection.

Breeding: The first successful breeding attempts were reported in the United States

during the 1960s and 1970s. The courtship probably starts with the female. Before copulation she performs a kind of courtship dance in which she hops from one leg to the other. The clutch consists of an average of two eggs. Brooding lasts from 29 to 30 days. The nestling period extends for 80 to 100 days.

As Companions: Umbrella cockatoos are probably too loud and destructive for most apartments and closely spaced dwellings. Males can be as unpredictable as teenagers; females probably make better long-term companions.

Moluccan Cockatoo
Cacatua moluccensis

Description: Total length 21½ inches (55 cm). Male: basic plumage color white, often with pinkish tinge; with pink covert feathers covering a large orange-red recumbent crest; beak black; legs gray; iris black. Female: similar to male but iris can be deep brown.

Distribution: Moluccan Islands Seram, Saparua, and Haruku, introduced to Ambon Island.

Habitat: Forested areas near the coast, principally low areas and hilly country under 3,280 feet (1000 m); in small flocks.

Maintenance: The largest cockatoos available commercially. They are best maintained in pairs in an outdoor aviary at least 6 feet (2 m) wide and with plenty of opportunity for exercise and occupation. Some birds can even be kept on a climbing tree when their wing feathers are well clipped (see page 35).

Breeding: A number of Moluccan cockatoos have been hand-raised in Europe, England, and the United States. The sensitive nature of the bird, the difficulty in establishing a pair, the need for huge quarters, and the price of acquiring two birds considerably increase the difficulty of attempting to breed Moluccan

cockatoos. The clutch usually consists of two to three eggs. The brooding period lasts 28 to 30 days. The nestling period extends for approximately 90 days.

As Companions: Their piercingly loud cries, destructive beak strength, and size, among other characteristics, make them difficult to keep as companions, especially in apartments and closely spaced dwellings. Moluccan cockatoos are very sensitive animals and can easily become feather pickers.

Less-Common Cockatoo Species

The popularity of cockatoo species kept as pets has changed over time. Years ago, the availability of a cockatoo species was determined mainly by the number of birds brought out of the wild. Now breeders are responsible for producing all pet cockatoos available in the United States. Breeders have selected the cockatoo species with the most appealing pet qualities and make those birds available to qualified pet owners.

One of the most striking cockatoo species is the Palm cockatoo (*Probosciger aterrimus*). These majestic dark-gray to black birds with the bright-red cheek patches have been slow to become established in aviculture because they were protected from export in their native lands of Australia and New Guinea. This species also produces only a single egg a year. This is in contrast to other cockatoo species that produce two or three eggs, providing breeders with a chance to rear "extra" chicks while the parent birds concentrate on one chick, usually the first one that hatched. Palm cockatoos are social, generally peaceful birds.

Another less-common cockatoo species is the Bare-eyed cockatoo (*Cacatua sanguinea*). These medium-sized white birds have bluish-gray bare eye rings that give them their common name. Bare-eyeds are native to Australia and New Guinea. They can be quick studies when learning to talk, but their voices are often loud. Bare-eyeds can be mischievous birds with a tendency toward obesity if not fed a varied, low-fat diet.

Some cockatoo species are so unusual that they almost take your breath away when you see them for the first time. Such can be the case with the Major Mitchell's or Leadbeater's cockatoo (*Cacatua leadbeateri*). These large pink birds with banded pink, yellow, and white crest feathers are found throughout inland Australia. They can be cuddly pets when young but require an observant owner and a consistent routine to prevent them from becoming demanding pets as adults.

INFORMATION

Books

Athan, Mattie Sue. *Guide to the Well-Behaved Parrot*, Hauppauge, NY: Barron's Educational Series, Inc., 2007.

_____. *Guide to Companion Parrot Behavior*, Hauppauge, NY: Barron's Educational Series, Inc., 2009.

Bergman, Petra. *Feeding Your Pet Bird*, Hauppauge, NY: Barron's Educational Series, Inc., 1993.

Doane, Bonnie Munro. *Parrot Training*, New York, NY: Howell Book House, 2001.

Harrison, Greg J., CVM, and Linda R. Harrison, BS. *Clinical Avian Medicine and Surgery*, Philadelphia, PA: W.B. Saunders Company, 1986.

Jupiter, Tony, and Mike Parr. *Parrots: A Guide to Parrots of the World*, New Haven, CT: Yale University Press, 1998.

Murphy, James J. *Cockatoos Are Different Because They Have Crests*, Gilbert, PA: White Mountain Bird Farm, Inc., 1998.

Ritchie, Branson, and Greg J. Harrison. A*vian Medicine: Principles and Application*, Lake Worth, FL: Wingers Publishing, Inc., 1997.

Organizations

American Federation of Aviculture
P.O. Box 91717
Austin, TX 78709
(512) 585-9800
email: *afaoffice@earthlink.net*

Association of Avian Veterinarians
P.O. Box 811720
Boca Raton, FL 33481
(561) 393-8901
email: *aavctrlofc@aol.com*

The Gabriel Foundation
1025 Acoma Street
Denver, CO 80204
(303) 629-5900
www.thegabrielfoundation.org

International Aviculturists Society
P.O. Box 341852
Memphis, TN 38184
www.FunnyFarmexotics.com/IAS/

The Oasis Sanctuary
P.O. Box 2166
Scottsdale, AZ 85252
www.the-oasis.org

World Parrot Trust
P.O. Box 935
Lake Alfred, FL 33850
info@worldparrottrust.org

INDEX

About the Authors

Werner Lantermann has been director of a private institute for parrot research in Oberhausen, Germany, since 1981. His specialty is the large parrots of South and Central America. He is the author of numerous articles in professional journals and successful books about parrotkeeping and breeding, among them Barron's *The New Parrot Handbook* and *Amazon Parrots*.

Susanne Lantermann is a co-worker in the private institute for parrot research in Oberhausen, Germany, and co-author of numerous books about African and South American parrots.

Julie Mancini has owned and cared for parrots for the past 20 years. She has been a freelance writer since 1997, with pets as her primary focus. A former editor of *Bird Talk* magazine, Julie is the author of 16 books and numerous articles on companion animal care.

Photo Credits

All photos by Joan Balzarini.

Cover Photos

Shutterstock: front cover, back cover, inside front cover, inside back cover.

English translation © copyright 2010, 2000, 1989 by Barron's Educational Series, Inc.
© Copyright 1988 by Gräfe und Unzer GmbH, Munich, Germany.
Original title of the German book is *Kakadus*.
Translated from the German by Elizabeth D. Crawford.

All inquiries should be addressed to:
Barron's Educational Series, Inc.
250 Wireless Boulevard
Hauppauge, NY 11788
www.barronseduc.com

ISBN-13: 987-0-7641-4346-5
ISBN-10: 0-7641-4346-8

Library of Congress Control Number: 2010925444

Printed in China

9 8 7 6 5 4 3 2 1

Your bird's everyday care starts with BARRON's

Barron's offers a variety of handsome and informative books on birds and bird care. Each manual and handbook has been individually written by an experienced breeder, vet, or ornithologist, and is filled with full-color photos and instructive, high-quality line art. You'll find everything you need to know about feeding, caging, breeding, and keeping healthy and contented birds.

Owner's Manuals   Each book, paperback, $8.99, Can$10.99

African Grey Parrots
ISBN 978-0-7641-1035-1

Amazon Parrots
ISBN 978-0-7641-4341-0

Budgerigars
ISBN 978-0-7641-3897-3

Caiques
ISBN 978-0-7641-3446-3

Canaries
ISBN 978-0-7641-4430-1

Cockatiels
ISBN 978-0-7641-3896-6

Cockatoos
ISBN 978-0-7641-4346-5

Conures
ISBN 978-0-7641-4366-3

Doves
ISBN 978-0-7641-3232-2

Eclectus Parrots
ISBN 978-0-7641-1886-9

Gouldian Finches
ISBN 978-0-7641-3850-8

Long-Tailed Parakeets
ISBN 978-0-8120-1351-1

Lovebirds
ISBN 978-0-7641-3062-5

Macaws
ISBN 978-0-7641-1920-0

Parakeets
ISBN 978-0-7641-1032-0

Parrots
ISBN 978-0-7641-2096-1

Pigeons
ISBN 978-0-7641-2991-9

The Second-Hand Parrot
ISBN 978-0-7641-1918-7

Zebra Finches
ISBN 978-0-7641-1040-5

Handbooks   Each book, paperback, $12.99, Can$15.99

The African Grey Parrot Handbook
ISBN 978-0-7641-4140-9

The Canary Handbook
ISBN 978-0-7641-1760-2

The Cockatiel Handbook
ISBN 978-0-7641-4292-5

The Conure Handbook
ISBN 978-0-7641-2783-0

The Finch Handbook
ISBN 978-0-7641-1826-5

The Lovebird Handbook
ISBN 978-0-7641-1827-2

The Parakeet Handbook
ISBN 978-0-7641-1018-4

The New Parrot Handbook
ISBN 978-0-8120-3729-6

The Parrotlet Handbook
ISBN 978-0-7641-4189-8

To order visit
www.barronseduc.com
or your local book store

Barron's Educational Series, Inc.
250 Wireless Blvd.
Hauppauge, N.Y. 11788
Order toll-free: 1-800-645-3476

In Canada:
Georgetown Book Warehouse
34 Armstrong Ave.
Georgetown, Ontario L7G 4R9
Canadian orders: 1-800-247-7160

Prices subject to change without notice.

(62b) 6/10